Simply Seder

A Passover Haggadah

Turn over for Planning Your Passover Seder

Edited by Dena Neusner
Illustrated by Julie Wohl

Editorial Committee:

Rabbi William Cutter
Sarah Gluck
Rabbi Lauren Kurland
Rabbi Mark Levine
Ellen J. Rank
Judith Sandman

BEHRMAN HOUSE
www.behrmanhouse.com/passover

EDITOR AND PROJECT MANAGER: Dena Neusner

ILLUSTRATOR: Julie Wohl

DESIGNER: Stacey May

Library of Congress Cataloging-in-Publication Data

Haggadah. English & Hebrew.
　　Simply seder : a Passover Haggadah / edited by Dena Neusner ; illustrated by
Julie Wohl.
　　　　p. cm.
　　"The book will be double-sided, with two front covers--one for the Haggadah
(opens from the right) and the other for the planning section (regular English
opening, from the left)"--Data view.
　　Text in Hebrew and romanized Hebrew, with English translation; planning
section in English.
　　ISBN 978-0-87441-883-5
　1.　Haggadot--Texts. 2.　Seder--Liturgy--Texts 3.　Judaism--Liturgy--Texts. 4.
Haggadah. 5.　Passover--Customs and practices. 6.　Jewish families--Religious life.
I. Neusner, Dena. II. Title.
　　BM674.643.N48 2011
　　296.4'5371--dc23

　　　　　　　　　　　　　　　　　　　2011026348

 Visit **www.behrmanhouse.com/passover** for blessings, songs, recipes, activities,
and games.

The Passover Seder

Tonight we gather for stories and songs, food and drink, and traditions both ancient and modern. We'll use all our senses to experience the Israelites' momentous journey from slavery to freedom.

The Passover seder as we know it has evolved from generation to generation, and it falls to each of us at this table to help tell the story of our ancestors' Exodus from Egypt.

Why do we have a Passover seder and retell the story each year? The story, rituals, and customs of the seder link us to previous generations and to the generations to come, and remind us of our responsibility to promote freedom and dignity. As we are inspired by the story of the Exodus and the wisdom of our sages, we add our own voices to the traditions of our people. What new traditions might you add to the seder this year?

The Seder Plate

The objects on the seder plate help us remember the Passover story:

Karpas כַּרְפַּס
A green vegetable (many use parsley) reminds us of spring. Some families follow a tradition of using a potato.

Beitzah בֵּיצָה
A roasted egg reminds us of the festival sacrifices that our ancestors offered at the Temple in Jerusalem.

Maror מָרוֹר
A bitter herb, usually horseradish, symbolizes the bitterness of slavery.

Zeroa זְרוֹעַ
A roasted bone, traditionally a lamb shank bone, reminds us of the animal sacrifice that our ancestors brought to the Temple in Jerusalem on Passover. Some vegetarians use a roasted beet instead, which has a deep red color that resembles the blood of the Temple sacrifice.

Charoset חֲרוֹסֶת

A mixture of fruit, wine, and nuts reminds us of the mortar and bricks that Pharaoh forced the Israelite slaves to make.

Chazeret חֲזֶרֶת

A second bitter herb, such as romaine lettuce, may also be put on the seder plate to remind us of the bitterness of slavery.

Some families place an orange on the seder plate as a symbol of how it is fruitful to fully include all members of the Jewish community at our holiday table and in Jewish life.

What other symbols would you add to the seder plate, and why?

Candle Lighting

We begin with the light and warmth of the holiday candles.

We light the candles and then recite the blessing. (On Shabbat, we add the words in parentheses.)

בָּרוּךְ אַתָּה יְיָ אֱלֹהֵינוּ מֶלֶךְ הָעוֹלָם, אֲשֶׁר קִדְּשָׁנוּ בְּמִצְוֹתָיו וְצִוָּנוּ לְהַדְלִיק נֵר שֶׁל (שַׁבָּת וְשֶׁל) יוֹם טוֹב.

Baruch Atah Adonai Eloheinu Melech ha'olam, asher kid'shanu b'mitzvotav v'tzivanu l'hadlik neir shel (Shabbat v'shel) yom tov.

Praised are You, Adonai our God, Ruler of the universe, whose commandments sanctify us and who has commanded us to light the (Shabbat and) festival candles.

Shehecheyanu

With the Shehecheyanu blessing, we express our thanks for having reached this moment, as we come together to celebrate Passover.

בָּרוּךְ אַתָּה יְיָ אֱלֹהֵינוּ מֶלֶךְ הָעוֹלָם, שֶׁהֶחֱיָנוּ וְקִיְּמָנוּ וְהִגִּיעָנוּ לַזְּמַן הַזֶּה.

Baruch Atah Adonai Eloheinu Melech ha'olam, shehecheyanu, v'kiy'manu, v'higi'anu laz'man hazeh.

Praised are You, Adonai our God, Ruler of the universe, who has given us life, sustained us, and brought us to this moment.

Order of the Seder

The word *seder* means "order." The ancient rabbis composed a particular order for the seder service, with a list of steps that we follow to this day. While we are encouraged to vary and expand on the service, every seder traditionally shares these same basic steps:

The Blessing over Wine — *Kadeish* קַדֵּשׁ

Washing Our Hands — *Ur'chatz* וּרְחַץ

Dipping the Greens in Salt Water — *Karpas* כַּרְפַּס

Breaking the Middle Matzah — *Yachatz* יַחַץ

Telling the Passover Story — *Magid* מַגִּיד

Washing Our Hands — *Rochtzah* רָחְצָה

Eating Matzah — *Motzi Matzah* מוֹצִיא מַצָּה

The Bitter Herbs  — *Maror* מָרוֹר

The Hillel Sandwich — *Koreich* כּוֹרֵךְ

The Festive Meal 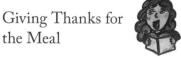 — *Shulchan Oreich* שֻׁלְחָן עוֹרֵךְ

The Afikoman — *Tzafun* צָפוּן

Giving Thanks for the Meal — *Bareich* בָּרֵךְ

Psalms of Praise — *Hallel* הַלֵּל

Completing the Seder 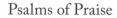 — *Nirtzah* נִרְצָה

The Blessing over Wine ◈ קַדֵּשׁ

Wine is a symbol of joy. Tonight we will drink four cups of wine. In the Torah, God makes four promises of deliverance to the Jewish people.

We raise our first cup of wine and read together the first of the four promises:

"I am Adonai, and I will free you from slavery in Egypt." (Exodus 6:6)

We say the blessing:

בָּרוּךְ אַתָּה יְיָ אֱלֹהֵינוּ מֶלֶךְ הָעוֹלָם, בּוֹרֵא פְּרִי הַגָּפֶן.

Baruch Atah Adonai Eloheinu Melech ha'olam, borei p'ri hagafen.

Praised are You, Adonai our God, Ruler of the universe, who creates the fruit of the vine.

Praised are You, Adonai our God, Ruler of the universe, who makes us holy through Your commandments. With love, You have given us (Shabbat for rest,) times for rejoicing, joyous festivals and holidays. You have given us (this Shabbat and) this Festival of Matzot, a celebration of our freedom from slavery in Egypt. Praised are you, Adonai, who sanctifies (Shabbat,) the people Israel, and the festival seasons.

We drink the first cup of wine, while reclining, with soft pillows on our chairs.

Washing Our Hands ◈ וּרְחַץ

Washing our hands helps us feel ready for the seder, rinsing away impurities along with the concerns and preoccupations of the day.

Participants take turns pouring water over both hands, either at the sink or at the table with a pitcher of water and a bowl. No blessing is said at this time.

Dipping the Greens in Salt Water ◈ כַּרְפַּס

Karpas, in the form of parsley or another green vegetable, reminds us that springtime is here, as it was when the Israelites left Egypt. We dip the karpas in salt water to remember the tears our ancestors shed as slaves for Pharaoh.

We dip the greens in salt water and recite the blessing.

בָּרוּךְ אַתָּה יְיָ אֱלֹהֵינוּ מֶלֶךְ הָעוֹלָם, בּוֹרֵא פְּרִי הָאֲדָמָה.

Baruch Atah Adonai Eloheinu Melech ha'olam, borei p'ri ha'adamah.

Praised are You, Adonai our God, Ruler of the universe, who creates the fruit of the earth.

We eat the karpas.

Breaking the Middle Matzah ◈ יַחַץ

The leader uncovers the plate with three matzot (plural of matzah), holds up the middle matzah for all to see, and breaks it in two.

We now break the middle matzah as a reminder that redemption is not complete as long as there is injustice and suffering in the world. We will designate the larger of the two broken pieces as the afikoman, and after dinner we will share it as a reminder that we can each do our part to bring about a better world.

The leader returns the smaller piece of matzah to the middle, then wraps the larger part and sets it aside. This piece is the afikoman, which the leader should hide (or designate someone else to hide) for the children to find during the meal.

"God seeks justice for the orphan and the widow, and cares for the stranger, providing the stranger with food and clothing. You, too, must show concern for the stranger, for you were strangers in the land of Egypt." (Deuteronomy 10:18-19)

At Passover we speak about welcoming the stranger. How can our own historical experience as strangers help us show true concern and love for those who are not part of our community?

הָא לַחְמָא עַנְיָא דִי אֲכָלוּ אַבְהָתָנָא בְּאַרְעָא דְמִצְרָיִם.

Ha lachma anya di achalu avhatana b'ara d'Mitzrayim.

This is the bread of poverty that our ancestors ate in the land of Egypt. Let all who are hungry come and eat with us. Let all who are in need come and celebrate Passover with us. Now we are here; next year may we be in the Land of Israel. Now we are slaves; next year may we be truly free.

We refill our wine cups.

This passage, Ha Lachma Anya, is written in Aramaic, the language of the Jewish people at the time the haggadah was composed. This reminds us that when we welcome the stranger, we invite our guest in the language he or she will understand.

The Four Questions

Asking questions is a sign of freedom. Traditionally the youngest child at the table reads or sings the Four Questions. Even if there are no children at the table, we still recite the Four Questions, as we continue a lifelong process of learning through questioning.

מַה נִּשְׁתַּנָּה הַלַּיְלָה הַזֶּה מִכָּל הַלֵּילוֹת?

שֶׁבְּכָל הַלֵּילוֹת אָנוּ אוֹכְלִין חָמֵץ וּמַצָּה. הַלַּיְלָה הַזֶּה כֻּלּוֹ מַצָּה.

שֶׁבְּכָל הַלֵּילוֹת אָנוּ אוֹכְלִין שְׁאָר יְרָקוֹת. הַלַּיְלָה הַזֶּה מָרוֹר.

שֶׁבְּכָל הַלֵּילוֹת אֵין אָנוּ מַטְבִּילִין אֲפִילוּ פַּעַם אֶחָת. הַלַּיְלָה הַזֶּה שְׁתֵּי פְּעָמִים.

שֶׁבְּכָל הַלֵּילוֹת אָנוּ אוֹכְלִין בֵּין יוֹשְׁבִין וּבֵין מְסֻבִּין. הַלַּיְלָה הַזֶּה כֻּלָּנוּ מְסֻבִּין.

Although we traditionally refer to this passage, Mah Nishtanah, as the Four Questions, it's actually worded as one question with four different aspects to it. What other questions do *you* have about the Passover seder?

***Mah nishtanah** halailah hazeh mikol haleilot?*

Sheb'chol haleilot anu och'lin chameitz umatzah.
Halailah hazeh kulo matzah.

Sheb'chol haleilot anu och'lin sh'ar y'rakot.
Halailah hazeh maror.

Sheb'chol haleilot ein anu matbilin afilu pa'am echat.
Halailah hazeh sh'tei f'amim.

Sheb'chol haleilot anu och'lin bein yoshvin uvein m'subin.
Halailah hazeh kulanu m'subin.

Why is this night different from all other nights?

1. On all other nights we eat either leavened or unleavened bread, but on this night we eat only matzah, unleavened bread.

2. On all other nights we eat all kinds of herbs, but on this night we eat only bitter herbs.

3. On all other nights we do not dip herbs even once, but on this night we dip twice.

4. On all other nights we eat either sitting or reclining, but on this night we all recline.

🌐 Visit **www.behrmanhouse.com/passover** to practice the Four Questions.

Telling the Passover Story ◈ מַגִּיד

So why *is* this night different from all other nights?
On this night we celebrate one of the most important
moments in the history of the Jewish people, when
we went forth from slavery to freedom. But before we
retell the story, let's answer the questions:

1. We eat only matzah to remember how our
    ancestors fled Egypt in such a hurry that they did
    not even have time for their bread dough to rise. Instead, the hot
    sun baked it into a flat, unleavened bread.

2. We eat bitter herbs to remind ourselves of how our ancestors' lives were
    made bitter as slaves in Egypt.

3. We dip karpas in salt water to remember the salty tears of the slaves,
    and we dip maror in sweet charoset to remember how the bitterness of
    slavery was sweetened by the hope for freedom.

4. We recline at the table as a symbol of freedom, because in ancient
    times, nobles and wealthy people would recline in comfort while they
    ate, while slaves could not.

Avadim Hayinu

We say or sing:

עֲבָדִים הָיִינוּ, הָיִינוּ, עַתָּה
בְּנֵי־חוֹרִין, בְּנֵי־חוֹרִין.

*Avadim hayinu, hayinu. Atah b'nei chorin,
b'nei chorin.*

We were slaves to Pharaoh in Egypt, but
Adonai our God brought us out of there
with a strong hand and an outstretched
arm. If God had not brought our
ancestors out of Egypt, then we and our
children and our children's children might still
be slaves. Therefore, even if we were all wise, even if we were all insightful
and learned in Torah, it would still be our duty to tell and retell the story
of the Exodus from Egypt. The more we tell the story of the Exodus, the
more we are to be praised. The more we reflect on the story, the deeper
will be our understanding of what freedom means, and the stronger our
determination to fight for freedom for ourselves and for others.

For generations we have told and retold the story of Passover. A tale is told
about five rabbis who were feasting at a seder table in the Land of Israel.
They became so engrossed in the story of the Exodus from Egypt that before
they knew it, their students came and called to them, "Rabbis, dawn is here.
It is time to say the morning Sh'ma: it is time for the morning prayers."

Think of a time when you became so absorbed in a story that you lost track
of time. What made the story so compelling? What aspects of the Passover
seder are most compelling to you?

The Four Children

As we retell the story of the Exodus from Egypt, we recognize that each of us learns differently and therefore must be told the story in a different way. The ancient rabbis spoke of four different kinds of children to whom the story is told.

The wise child asks, "What are the laws and rules that God has commanded?" This child loves Passover and is eager to understand the significance of the holiday. We teach this child the customs and rituals of Passover, and we explain how our traditions remind us of the importance of freedom for all people.

The defiant child asks, "What does this service mean to you?" With the words "to you" this child speaks as an outsider, separate from the seder and from the community. We challenge this child, saying, "This is because of what God did for *me* when I went out of Egypt. For me, not for you. Because you set yourself apart from the Jewish people, you would not have made the journey from slavery to freedom."

The simple child asks, "What is this all about?" This child does not understand the holiday but would like to know more. We reassure this child with a simple answer, "With a strong hand, God brought us out of Egypt, from the house of slavery."

The fourth child does not even know how to ask. We awaken this child's interest and gently explain, "This is because of what God did for me when I went out of Egypt."

The sage Ben Zoma said, "Who is wise? The one who learns from every person." (Pirkei Avot 4:1) The wise child, as described by the rabbis, wants to know all the facts and details of the seder. How is this different from Ben Zoma's definition of wisdom? What do you think makes someone wise?

Is it fair to characterize the second child as defiant? Why do you think this child acts this way?

In what circumstances are you most like each of these four children?

The Passover Story

There are many ways to tell the Passover story. Participants may read it aloud, take turns telling it in their own words, or even act it out.

In ancient times, our ancestors worshipped idols, until one man, Abraham, rejected idols and came to worship one God. Abraham and his wife Sarah traveled to Canaan, as the Land of Israel was called, where God made a promise that their children would become a great nation.

Our people came to Egypt, where they lived in peace for generations. Then a Pharaoh came to power who feared that the Israelites, as our ancestors were called, would increase in number until they rose up against him. Pharaoh made them slaves and embittered their lives with hard labor: making bricks and mortar, and building cities. Then he decreed that all Israelite baby boys should be drowned in the Nile River.

וְהִיא שֶׁעָמְדָה לַאֲבוֹתֵינוּ וְלָנוּ.

V'hi she'amdah la'avoteinu v'lanu.

God's promise has been a source of strength to our ancestors and to us. For not only did the Egyptians try to destroy us, but in every generation enemies have risen up against us, and God has saved us from their hands.

Surprisingly, Moses is not really mentioned in the traditional haggadah, although he looms large in the story of the Exodus in the Torah. The sages may have omitted Moses in order to emphasize that it was God who redeemed us from Egypt, not Moses. Another explanation says that any one of us can have an individual relationship with God and help to change the world. Why do you think Moses was omitted from the traditional haggadah?

One Israelite woman hid her son to keep him alive. She placed him in a basket in the Nile River and the boy's sister, Miriam, went to watch over him. Pharaoh's daughter came to bathe in the river and found the basket. She adopted the baby and named him Moses, which means "drawn from the water."

Moses grew up in the luxury of Pharaoh's palace. But he could not ignore the suffering of his people. One day he saw an Egyptian beating an Israelite slave, and in anger he killed the Egyptian. Fearing for his life, Moses fled from Egypt and settled in the land of Midian, where he became a shepherd.

Years later, Moses saw a bush that burned without being consumed. God spoke to Moses from the bush, saying, "I am the God of your ancestors, and I have seen the suffering of your people." God commanded Moses to return to Egypt and lead the Israelites to freedom.

"Let My People Go"
(From an African American spiritual)
When Israel was in Egypt's land,
Let my people go.
Oppressed so hard they could not stand,
Let my people go.
Go down, Moses, way down in Egypt's land.
Tell old Pharaoh to let my people go.

Moses and his brother Aaron went to Pharaoh and demanded that he free the Israelites. But Pharaoh refused, and instead made the slaves work even harder. So God brought terrible plagues upon the land—blood, frogs, lice, wild beasts, cattle disease, boils, hail, locusts, and darkness. Though his own people suffered from these plagues, Pharaoh's heart remained hardened.

Then came the tenth and most terrible plague. Every firstborn Egyptian died. Only the Israelites were spared. A great cry rose up from Egypt, and Pharaoh finally agreed to let the Israelites go free.

The Ten Plagues
As we name each of the ten plagues brought upon Egypt, we dip a spoon or finger into our cups and remove a drop of wine onto our plates. By lessening our wine, we demonstrate that we do not rejoice in the suffering of our enemies, but rather that our own joy is diminished by it.

Blood	Dam דָּם
Frogs	Tz'fardei'a צְפַרְדֵּעַ
Lice	Kinim כִּנִּים
Wild beasts	Arov עָרוֹב
Cattle disease	Dever דֶּבֶר
Boils	Sh'chin שְׁחִין
Hail	Barad בָּרָד
Locusts	Arbeh אַרְבֶּה
Darkness	Choshech חֹשֶׁךְ
Death of the firstborn	Makat b'chorot מַכַּת בְּכוֹרוֹת

The Israelites left in a great hurry. Pharaoh soon changed his mind and sent his army after them. The army pursued them to the banks of the Sea of Reeds. God told Moses to raise his staff, and the waters separated, allowing the Israelites to cross through the dry seabed out of Egypt to safety on the other side. The Egyptians pursued them into the sea, but the waters rushed back upon the Egyptian soldiers, drowning them. Safely on the other side, Moses and the Israelites sang a song of praise to God. Then Moses's sister, Miriam, led the women in joyous song and dance.

And so began the Israelites' journey from slavery to freedom, from sadness to joy, from being strangers in Egypt to becoming a great nation.

Dayeinu

Throughout our history, God has given us many wonderful gifts. For each one, we say *Dayeinu*, "It would have been enough." How much more grateful we are, then, for *all* the many good things God has done for us!

We sing together:

Ilu hotzi'anu miMitzrayim, dayeinu.

אִלּוּ הוֹצִיאָנוּ מִמִּצְרַיִם, דַּיֵּנוּ.

Ilu natan lanu et haShabbat, dayeinu.

אִלּוּ נָתַן לָנוּ אֶת הַשַׁבָּת, דַּיֵּנוּ.

Ilu natan lanu et haTorah, dayeinu.

אִלּוּ נָתַן לָנוּ אֶת הַתּוֹרָה, דַּיֵּנוּ.

After the leader recites each verse, everyone responds "Dayeinu!"

Had God brought us out of Egypt and not divided the sea for us, *Dayeinu!*

Had God divided the sea for us and not led us through on dry land, *Dayeinu!*

Had God led us through on dry land and not cared for us in the desert for forty years, *Dayeinu!*

Had God cared for us in the desert for forty years and not fed us with manna, *Dayeinu!*

Had God fed us with manna and not given us Shabbat, *Dayeinu!*

Had God given us Shabbat and not brought us to Mount Sinai, *Dayeinu!*

Had God brought us to Mount Sinai and not given us the Torah, *Dayeinu!*

Had God given us the Torah and not brought us to the Land of Israel, *Dayeinu!*

Had God brought us to the land of Israel and not built the Temple for us, *Dayeinu!*

Make up your own "Dayeinu" poem or song. Each participant adds one thing in their own life for which they are thankful. Don't forget to say *Dayeinu!*

 Visit **www.behrmanhouse.com/passover** to hear "Dayeinu."

Pesach, Matzah, Maror

According to Rabban Gamliel, no seder is complete until *pesach*, *matzah*, and *maror* are explained.

The leader holds up the roasted bone or beet.

The **pesach**, a roasted bone or beet, reminds us of the Passover sacrifice that our ancestors brought to the Temple in Jerusalem to celebrate the Exodus from Egypt. It is called *pesach*, which means "pass over," because the Torah tells us that God passed over the houses of the Israelites in Egypt, sparing them when the Egyptians' firstborn were slain.

The leader holds up the matzah.

The **matzah**, or unleavened bread, is a symbol of the bread of poverty we ate when we were slaves in Egypt. It reminds us of how the Israelites fled from Egypt in such a hurry that they did not have time for their bread dough to rise.

The leader holds up the dish of maror.

The **maror**, or bitter herbs, reminds us of how the Egyptians made the lives of the Israelite slaves bitter with hard and degrading work.

In Every Generation

בְּכָל דוֹר וָדוֹר חַיָּב אָדָם לִרְאוֹת אֶת עַצְמוֹ
כְּאִלּוּ הוּא יָצָא מִמִּצְרָיִם.

B'chol dor vador chayav adam lirot et atzmo k'ilu hu yatza miMitzrayim.

In every generation, each of us must think of ourselves as though we personally came out of Egypt.

We raise our wine cups and say together:

We therefore sing praises and give thanks to Adonai, who performed wonders for our ancestors and for us. God brought us
from slavery to freedom,
from sorrow to joy,
from mourning to festivity,
from darkness to light,
and from slavery to redemption.
Let us sing a new song before God. Halleluyah!

We lower our cups and continue with a psalm praising God's powerful presence.

בְּצֵאת יִשְׂרָאֵל מִמִּצְרָיִם, בֵּית יַעֲקֹב מֵעַם לֹעֵז. הָיְתָה יְהוּדָה
לְקָדְשׁוֹ, יִשְׂרָאֵל מַמְשְׁלוֹתָיו. הַיָּם רָאָה וַיָּנֹס, הַיַּרְדֵּן יִסֹּב לְאָחוֹר.

B'tzeit Yisrael miMitzrayim, beit Ya'akov mei'am lo'eiz. Haitah Y'hudah l'kodsho, Yisrael mamsh'lotav. Hayam ra'ah vayanos, haYardein yisov l'achor.

When Israel came out of Egypt, the house of Jacob from a people of foreign speech, Judah became God's sanctuary, Israel God's dominion. The sea saw it and fled; the Jordan turned backward. The mountains skipped like rams, and the hills like lambs.

Why, O sea, do you flee? Why, O Jordan, do you turn backward? You mountains, why do you skip like rams, and you hills, like lambs? Earth, tremble at God's presence, at the presence of the God of Jacob, who turned the rock into a pool of water, the flint into a fountain.

(Psalm 114)

The Second Cup of Wine

We raise our second cup of wine and read together God's second promise of deliverance in the Torah.

"I will deliver you from slavery." (Exodus 6:6)

בָּרוּךְ אַתָּה יְיָ אֱלֹהֵינוּ מֶלֶךְ הָעוֹלָם, בּוֹרֵא פְּרִי הַגָּפֶן.

Baruch Atah Adonai Eloheinu Melech ha'olam, borei p'ri hagafen.

Praised are You, Adonai our God, Ruler of the universe, who creates the fruit of the vine.

We drink the second cup of wine.

Washing Our Hands ◈
רָחְצָה

We wash our hands and say the blessing.

בָּרוּךְ אַתָּה יְיָ אֱלֹהֵינוּ מֶלֶךְ הָעוֹלָם, אֲשֶׁר קִדְּשָׁנוּ בְּמִצְוֹתָיו וְצִוָּנוּ עַל נְטִילַת יָדָיִם.

Baruch Atah Adonai Eloheinu Melech ha'olam, asher kid'shanu b'mitzvotav v'tzivanu al n'tilat yadayim.

Praised are You, Adonai our God, Ruler of the universe, whose commandments sanctify us and who has commanded us to wash our hands.

Eating Matzah ◈ מוֹצִיא מַצָּה

The leader distributes pieces of the top and middle matzah to each participant. Before eating the matzah, we recite two blessings, one for food, which is the same blessing we say for bread, and another one specifically for matzah.

בָּרוּךְ אַתָּה יְיָ אֱלֹהֵינוּ מֶלֶךְ הָעוֹלָם, הַמּוֹצִיא לֶחֶם מִן הָאָרֶץ.

Baruch Atah Adonai Eloheinu Melech ha'olam, hamotzi lechem min ha'aretz.

Praised are You, Adonai our God, Ruler of the universe, who brings forth bread from the earth.

בָּרוּךְ אַתָּה יְיָ אֱלֹהֵינוּ מֶלֶךְ הָעוֹלָם, אֲשֶׁר קִדְּשָׁנוּ בְּמִצְוֹתָיו וְצִוָּנוּ עַל אֲכִילַת מַצָּה.

Baruch Atah Adonai Eloheinu Melech ha'olam, asher kid'shanu b'mitzvotav v'tzivanu al achilat matzah.

Praised are You, Adonai our God, Ruler of the universe, whose commandments sanctify us and who has commanded us to eat matzah.

The Bitter Herbs ❖ מָרוֹר

As we dip bitter herbs in sweet charoset we remember that our ancestors were able to bear the bitterness of slavery because of their hopeful and sweet thoughts of freedom.

We say the blessing and then eat the bitter herbs with charoset.

בָּרוּךְ אַתָּה יְיָ אֱלֹהֵינוּ מֶלֶךְ הָעוֹלָם, אֲשֶׁר קִדְּשָׁנוּ בְּמִצְוֹתָיו וְצִוָּנוּ עַל אֲכִילַת מָרוֹר.

Baruch Atah Adonai Eloheinu Melech ha'olam, asher kid'shanu b'mitzvotav v'tzivanu al achilat maror.

Praised are You, Adonai our God, Ruler of the universe, whose commandments sanctify us and who has commanded us to eat bitter herbs.

The Hillel Sandwich ❖ כּוֹרֵךְ

The leader distributes pieces from the bottom matzah, along with portions of maror and charoset, for the Hillel sandwich.

In the days of the Temple in Jerusalem, the great teacher Hillel used to make a sandwich of matzah and maror with the Pesach lamb. He ate it to fulfill the biblical command, "You shall eat [the Passover sacrifice] with matzah and maror." (Numbers 9:11) Today, we eat a Hillel sandwich, composed of matzah and bitter herbs, often with charoset added, thus combining symbols of slavery and of freedom.

We eat the Hillel sandwich. No blessing is recited.

Rabbi Hillel said, "If I am not for myself, who will be for me? But if I am only for myself, what am I? And if not now, when?" (Pirkei Avot 1:14)

How is this famous quote from our tradition relevant to the Passover story? What does Hillel mean by each of these three questions?

The Festive Meal ◈ שֻׁלְחָן עוֹרֵךְ

Time to eat!

The Afikoman ◈ צָפוּן

After the meal, the children search for the hidden matzah, the afikoman. The leader gives a reward in exchange for the afikoman, and everyone eats a piece of it for dessert. After we eat the afikoman, our seder continues.

Rabban Shimon Ben Gamliel said: "The world stands on three things: On truth, on justice, and on peace." (Pirkei Avot 1:18)

As we share the afikoman, we reflect on the words of Rabban Gamliel. What does he mean when he says that the world stands on these three things? How can we work together to promote these values at home and around the world?

Giving Thanks for the Meal ◈ בָּרֵךְ

We say or sing Birkat Hamazon, the blessing after the meal.

בָּרוּךְ אַתָּה יְיָ אֱלֹהֵינוּ מֶלֶךְ הָעוֹלָם, הַזָּן אֶת הָעוֹלָם כֻּלוֹ בְּטוּבוֹ בְּחֵן בְּחֶסֶד וּבְרַחֲמִים. הוּא נוֹתֵן לֶחֶם לְכָל בָּשָׂר כִּי לְעוֹלָם חַסְדּוֹ. וּבְטוּבוֹ הַגָּדוֹל תָּמִיד לֹא חָסַר לָנוּ, וְאַל יֶחְסַר לָנוּ מָזוֹן לְעוֹלָם וָעֶד בַּעֲבוּר שְׁמוֹ הַגָּדוֹל, כִּי הוּא אֵל זָן וּמְפַרְנֵס לַכֹּל וּמֵטִיב לַכֹּל, וּמֵכִין מָזוֹן לְכָל בְּרִיּוֹתָיו אֲשֶׁר בָּרָא. בָּרוּךְ אַתָּה, יְיָ, הַזָּן אֶת הַכֹּל.

Baruch Atah Adonai Eloheinu Melech ha'olam, hazan et ha'olam kulo b'tuvo b'chein b'chesed uv'rachamim. Hu notein lechem l'chol basar ki l'olam chasdo. Uv'tuvo hagadol tamid lo chasar lanu, v'al yechsar lanu mazon l'olam va'ed ba'avur sh'mo hagadol, ki hu El zan um'farneis lakol umeitiv lakol, umeichin mazon l'chol b'riyotav asher bara. Baruch Atah, Adonai, hazan et hakol.

Praised are You, Adonai our God, Ruler of the universe, who provides for the entire world with goodness and grace, with kindness and with mercy.

You give food to all people; Your kindness endures forever.

Because of Your great goodness we have never lacked sustenance, nor shall we ever lack sustenance in the future because of Your great name.

You support and sustain all creatures and bring goodness to all, providing food for all creation.

Praised are You, Adonai, Provider for all.

The Third Cup of Wine

We raise our third cup of wine and read together God's third promise of deliverance in the Torah.

"I will redeem you with an outstretched arm."
(Exodus 6:6)

בָּרוּךְ אַתָּה יְיָ אֱלֹהֵינוּ מֶלֶךְ הָעוֹלָם, בּוֹרֵא פְּרִי הַגָּפֶן.

Baruch Atah Adonai Eloheinu Melech ha'olam, borei p'ri hagafen.

Praised are You, Adonai our God, Ruler of the universe, Creator of the fruit of the vine.

We drink the third cup of wine.

Welcoming Elijah

The leader points to the cup of wine reserved for the prophet Elijah.

This is called Elijah's Cup. Tradition teaches that the prophet Elijah is the messenger who will usher in a time of peace and freedom. We can each add a little wine from our own cup to Elijah's Cup. This reminds us that we all must contribute in order to create a better world.

The leader asks a participant, usually a child, to open the door of the home to welcome Elijah, and then we sing:

אֵלִיָּהוּ הַנָּבִיא, אֵלִיָּהוּ הַתִּשְׁבִּי, אֵלִיָּהוּ, אֵלִיָּהוּ, אֵלִיָּהוּ הַגִּלְעָדִי,
בִּמְהֵרָה בְיָמֵינוּ יָבֹא אֵלֵינוּ עִם מָשִׁיחַ בֶּן דָּוִד.

Eliyahu hanavi, Eliyahu haTishbi, Eliyahu, Eliyahu, Eliyahu haGiladi,
Bimheirah v'yameinu yavo eileinu, im Mashiach ben David.

Elijah the prophet, Elijah the Tishbite, Elijah, Elijah, Elijah from Gilead,
Quickly in our days may he come to us with the Messiah, son of David.

Rabbi Tarfon taught: "It is not your responsibility to finish the work [of perfecting the world], but you are not free to desist from it either." (Pirkei Avot 2:21)

How can each of us work toward perfecting the world? What does Rabbi Tarfon mean when he says "it is not your responsibility to finish the work"?

 Visit **www.behrmanhouse.com/passover** to hear "Eliyahu Hanavi."

Miriam's Cup

The prophet Miriam watched over her brother Moses along the banks of the Nile, and later she inspired the people with song and dance after crossing the Sea of Reeds. Tradition teaches that a miraculous well followed Miriam until the day she died, providing the Israelites with fresh water in the desert. We fill Miriam's Cup with water to remember Miriam and to honor the contributions of other women from our history.

Psalms of Praise ◈ הַלֵּל

We fill the fourth cup of wine and recite Hallel, psalms of praise.

Praise God, all nations;
Praise God, all peoples!
For God's kindness overwhelms us,
And God's truth endures forever.
Halleluyah!

(Psalm 117)

If our mouths were as filled with song as the sea,
And our tongues with joy as the endless waves,
And our lips with praise as the wide expanse of the heavens;
If our eyes were as radiant as the sun and the moon,
And our hands were spread out like eagles' wings,
And our feet were swift as deer,
Yet we would be unable to thank you,
Our God and God of our ancestors,
For one small measure of the kindness you have shown to our ancestors
and to us.

(from Nishmat)

The Fourth Cup of Wine

We raise our fourth cup of wine and read together God's fourth promise of deliverance in the Torah.

"I will take you to be my people, and I will be your God." (Exodus 6:7)

בָּרוּךְ אַתָּה יְיָ אֱלֹהֵינוּ מֶלֶךְ הָעוֹלָם, בּוֹרֵא פְּרִי הַגָּפֶן.

Baruch Atah Adonai Eloheinu Melech ha'olam, borei p'ri hagafen.

Praised are You, Adonai our God, Ruler of the universe, who creates the fruit of the vine.

We drink the fourth cup of wine.

Echad Mi Yodei'a? ◆ Who Knows One?

Passover songs can be a memorable part of the seder. "Echad Mi Yodei'a" uses cumulative verses based on numbers to teach Jewish concepts.

Echad mi yodei'a? Echad ani yodei'a: *Echad Eloheinu shebashamayim uva'aretz.*

Sh'nayim mi yodei'a? Sh'nayim ani yodei'a: *Sh'nei luchot habrit, echad Eloheinu shebashamayim uva'aretz.*

Sh'loshah mi yodei'a? Sh'loshah ani yodei'a: *Sh'loshah avot, sh'nei luchot habrit, echad Eloheinu shebashamayim uva'aretz.*

Arba mi yodei'a? Arba ani yodei'a: *Arba imahot, sh'loshah avot, sh'nei luchot habrit, echad Eloheinu shebashamayim uva'aretz.*

Chamishah mi yodei'a? Chamishah ani yodei'a: *Chamishah chumshei Torah, arba imahot, sh'loshah avot, sh'nei luchot habrit, echad Eloheinu shebashamayim uva'aretz.*

Shishah mi yodei'a? Shishah ani yodei'a: *Shishah sidrei Mishnah, Chamishah chumshei Torah, arba imahot, sh'loshah avot, sh'nei luchot habrit, echad Eloheinu shebashamayim uva'aretz.*

Shiv'ah mi yodei'a? Shiv'ah ani yodei'a: *Shiv'ah y'mei Shabta, shishah sidrei Mishnah, chamishah chumshei Torah, arba imahot, sh'loshah avot, sh'nei luchot habrit, echad Eloheinu shebashamayim uva'aretz.*

Sh'monah mi yodei'a? Sh'monah ani yodei'a: *Sh'monah y'mei milah, shiv'ah y'mei Shabta, shishah sidrei Mishnah, chamishah chumshei Torah, arba imahot, sh'loshah avot, sh'nei luchot habrit, echad Eloheinu shebashamayim uva'aretz.*

Tish'ah mi yodei'a? Tish'ah ani yodei'a: *Tish'ah yarchei leidah, sh'monah y'mei milah, shiv'ah y'mei Shabta, shishah sidrei Mishnah, chamishah chumshei Torah, arba imahot, sh'loshah avot, sh'nei luchot habrit, echad Eloheinu shebashamayim uva'aretz.*

Asarah mi yodei'a? Asarah ani yodei'a: *Asarah dibraya, tish'ah yarchei leidah, sh'monah y'mei milah, shiv'ah y'mei Shabta, shishah sidrei Mishnah, chamishah chumshei Torah, arba imahot, sh'loshah avot, sh'nei luchot habrit, echad Eloheinu shebashamayim uva'aretz.*

Achad asar mi yodei'a? Achad asar ani yodei'a: Achad asar kochvaya, asarah dibraya, tish'ah yarchei leidah, sh'monah y'mei milah, shiv'ah y'mei Shabta, shishah sidrei Mishnah, chamishah chumshei Torah, arba imahot, sh'loshah avot, sh'nei luchot habrit, echad Eloheinu shebashamayim uva'aretz.

Sh'neim asar mi yodei'a? Sh'neim asar ani yodei'a: Sh'neim asar shivtaya, achad asar kochvaya, asarah dibraya, tish'ah yarchei leidah, sh'monah y'mei milah, shiv'ah y'mei Shabta, shishah sidrei Mishnah, chamishah chumshei Torah, arba imahot, sh'loshah avot, sh'nei luchot habrit, echad Eloheinu shebashamayim uva'aretz.

Sh'loshah asar mi yodei'a? Sh'loshah asar ani yodei'a: Sh'loshah asar midaya, sh'neim asar shivtaya, achad asar kochvaya, asarah dibraya, tish'ah yarchei leidah, sh'monah y'mei milah, shiv'ah y'mei Shabta, shishah sidrei Mishnah, chamishah chumshei Torah, arba imahot, sh'loshah avot, sh'nei luchot habrit, echad Eloheinu shebashamayim uva'aretz.

Who knows one? I know one: One is our God in heaven and on earth.

Who knows two? I know two: Two are the tablets of the law, and One is our God in heaven and on earth.

Who knows three? I know three: Three are the patriarchs, two are the tablets of the law, and One is our God in heaven and on earth.

Four are the matriarchs…
Five are the books of the Torah…
Six are the books of the Mishnah…
Seven are the days of the week…
Eight are the days until circumcision…
Nine are the months of pregnancy…
Ten are the Commandments…
Eleven are the stars in Joseph's dream…
Twelve are the tribes of Israel…
Thirteen are the attributes of God…

 Visit **www.behrmanhouse.com/passover** to hear popular seder songs.

Chad Gadya ◈ One Little Goat

This Aramaic folk song, constructed in a familiar cumulative style, is an allegory for the Jewish people's history. It refers to how the Land of Israel was conquered by the Assyrians and the Babylonians, who were in turn destroyed by the Persians, who were defeated by the Macedonians, and then by the Romans, and so on. It ends with the expression of hope that the Holy One will prevail and bring peace to the people of Israel.

Chad gadya, chad gadya, **dizvan aba bitrei zuzei, chad gadya, chad gadya.**

V'ata shunra, v'achlah l'gadya, **dizvan aba bitrei zuzei, chad gadya, chad gadya.**

V'ata chalba, v'nashach l'shunra, d'achlah l'gadya, **dizvan aba bitrei zuzei, chad gadya, chad gadya.**

V'ata chutra, v'hikah l'chalba, d'nashach l'shunra, d'achlah l'gadya, **dizvan aba bitrei zuzei, chad gadya, chad gadya.**

V'ata nura, v'saraf l'chutra, d'hikah l'chalba, d'nashach l'shunra, d'achlah l'gadya, **dizvan aba bitrei zuzei, chad gadya, chad gadya.**

V'ata maya, v'chavah l'nura, d'saraf l'chutra, d'hikah l'chalba, d'nashach l'shunra, d'achlah l'gadya, **dizvan aba bitrei zuzei, chad gadya, chad gadya.**

V'ata tora, v'shata l'maya, d'chavah l'nura, d'saraf l'chutra, d'hikah l'chalba, d'nashach l'shunra, d'achlah l'gadya, **dizvan aba bitrei zuzei, chad gadya, chad gadya.**

V'ata hashocheit, v'shachat l'tora, d'shata l'maya, d'chavah l'nura, d'saraf l'chutra, d'hikah l'chalba, d'nashach l'shunra, d'achlah l'gadya, **dizvan aba bitrei zuzei, chad gadya, chad gadya.**

V'ata malach hamavet, v'shachat lashocheit, d'shachat l'tora, d'shata l'maya, d'chavah l'nura, d'saraf l'chutra, d'hikah l'chalba, d'nashach l'shunra, d'achlah l'gadya, **dizvan aba bitrei zuzei, chad gadya, chad gadya.**

V'ata haKadosh Baruch Hu, v'shachat l'malach hamavet, d'shachat lashocheit, d'shachat l'tora, d'shata l'maya, d'chavah l'nura, d'saraf l'chutra, d'hikah l'chalba, d'nashach l'shunra, d'achlah l'gadya, **dizvan aba bitrei zuzei, chad gadya, chad gadya.**

One little goat, one little goat, my father bought for two zuzim, *chad gadya*, *chad gadya*.

Then came a cat and ate the goat my father bought for two zuzim, *chad gadya*, *chad gadya*.

Then came a dog and bit the cat that ate the goat my father bought for two zuzim, *chad gadya*, *chad gadya*.

Then came a stick and hit the dog that bit the cat that ate the goat my father bought for two zuzim, *chad gadya*, *chad gadya*.

Then came a fire and burned the stick that hit the dog that bit the cat that ate the goat my father bought for two zuzim, *chad gadya*, *chad gadya*.

Then came water and quenched the fire that burned the stick that hit the dog that bit the cat that ate the goat my father bought for two zuzim, *chad gadya*, *chad gadya*.

Then came an ox and drank the water that quenched the fire that burned the stick that hit the dog that bit the cat that ate the goat my father bought for two zuzim, *chad gadya*, *chad gadya*.

Then came a butcher and slaughtered the ox that drank the water that quenched the fire that burned the stick that hit the dog that bit the cat that ate the goat my father bought for two zuzim, *chad gadya*, *chad gadya*.

Then came the angel of death and killed the butcher that slaughtered the ox that drank the water that quenched the fire that burned the stick that hit the dog that bit the cat that ate the goat my father bought for two zuzim, *chad gadya*, *chad gadya*.

Then came the Holy One, praised be God, and destroyed the angel of death that killed the butcher that slaughtered the ox that drank the water that quenched the fire that burned the stick that hit the dog that bit the cat that ate the goat my father bought for two zuzim, *chad gadya*, *chad gadya*.

Completing the Seder ◈ נִרְצָה

We have come to the end of our seder. We have told the story of our people's journey from slavery to freedom. We rededicate ourselves to helping those who are not free or who are in need. Next year may there be freedom and peace for all people.

L'shanah haba'ah biY'rushalayim!

לְשָׁנָה הַבָּאָה בִּירוּשָׁלָיִם.

Next year in Jerusalem!

Why do we say "Next year in Jerusalem"? Originally these words represented the longing of Jews scattered around the world, in the Diaspora, to return to the Land of Israel. For some Jews today, the phrase may refer to spiritual redemption or the messianic longing for a rebuilt Temple in Jerusalem; for others, it is a way of expressing solidarity with Am Yisrael, the Jewish community past, present, and future. For some, the phrase encapsulates the wish that Jerusalem, and the modern State of Israel, will soon find a lasting peace; and for still others, it is a general expression of hope and desire for a brighter future for ourselves and for the world. What does "Next year in Jerusalem" mean to you?

Searching for Chameitz

It's the night before the first seder. The seder plate is ready, the service is planned, the children have been busy with activities and crafts, guests are making final travel plans, and the meal is under control. It's time for an age-old ritual that literally and spiritually prepares us for this Festival of Matzah.

Before Passover, we clean our house of all chameitz, or leavened foods, which we do not eat during the holiday. This includes foods that are allowed to rise, such as bread, pasta, or cookies. The night before the first seder, we symbolically search the house for chameitz, using a candle, a feather, and a wooden spoon.

This is a fun activity in which to involve children. First, hide a few small pieces of bread in advance. Then turn off the lights and invite children to search by candlelight (or flashlight, for safety). When they find chameitz, they can use the feather to brush it into the spoon and dispose of it. Then recite the following blessing:

בָּרוּךְ אַתָּה יְיָ אֱלֹהֵינוּ מֶלֶךְ הָעוֹלָם, אֲשֶׁר קִדְּשָׁנוּ בְּמִצְוֹתָיו, וְצִוָּנוּ
עַל בִּעוּר חָמֵץ.

Baruch Atah Adonai Eloheinu Melech ha'olam, asher kid'shanu b'mitzvotav v'tzivanu al bi'ur chameitz.

Praised are You, Adonai our God, Ruler of the universe, whose commandments sanctify us and who has commanded us to remove the chameitz.

The leavened chameitz can represent the puffed-up ego or selfishness that is in every one of us. We symbolically remove it from our lives as we approach the Passover seder, so that we may focus more fully on the ideas of freedom and tikun olam, repairing the world.

When you're ready, turn this book over for your Passover haggadah. Chag same'ach! Have a happy and meaningful holiday.

The Seder Service

Being familiar with the types of blessings, readings, and rituals in the haggadah will help you lead a meaningful and memorable seder. You might want to review the haggadah and consider the following questions before Passover:

Who will read?
Decide which parts you'll want to read aloud, and which parts you'll ask participants to read. Be sure to give everyone a turn to participate. Also think about how the Passover story itself will be told—will participants take turns reading the story *(from pages 18-21)* or telling it in their own words? Will children provide a creative telling, such as a skit or puppet show?

Hebrew, English, or both?
Transliterations are provided throughout, so anyone can read the Hebrew blessings and prayers.

How long will it last?
You can complete the seder in as little as 30 minutes if you choose, especially when there are young children present. For a richer, more meaningful experience, you can explore the discussion questions with your guests, or even provide additional stories and readings that have personal meaning.

How will you handle the afikoman?
Decide whether you will hide it yourself or designate someone else to do it, and what reward you'll offer to the participants (usually children) who look for it. *(See pages 10 and 29 of the haggadah)*.

How can you encourage participation from all guests?
Consider asking guests of all ages, in advance, to bring or prepare something to share at the seder table. Ideas might include:

- Some charoset, from their favorite recipe
- A dramatic retelling of the Passover story
- A musical performance
- A sing-along to popular seder songs
- Original artwork
- Family stories
- Family photos
- A discussion question

Activities for Children (and Adults, Too!)

The Passover seder has built-in roles for children, from asking the Four Questions to searching for the afikoman. You can also heighten anticipation by introducing Passover stories, themes, and projects in the days and weeks before Passover. The more you can involve your children in the seder, the more they will learn from and enjoy the experience.

Many of these ideas will appeal to adults as well.

❖ Help children plan a skit or song to tell the Passover story, and encourage them to perform it during the seder. Adults and older children can help organize younger ones or take on more challenging roles in the skit.

❖ Encourage children to make their own seder plate, matzah cover, and cups for Elijah and Miriam. They will love seeing their work proudly displayed on the seder table.

❖ Help children put together costumes or finger puppets to tell the story of Passover.

❖ Encourage children to practice the Four Questions from this haggadah or online, where they can hear the Mah Nishtanah chanted.

❖ Ask participants of all ages to come up with another four questions to share at the seder.

❖ Introduce the holiday to the youngest children with Passover picture books and games.

❖ Invite children to help search the house for chameitz, leavened bread, the night before the seder. (See page vii for more information.)

❖ Provide Passover-themed coloring pages, puzzles, and even bingo cards to hold children's interest during the seder.

❖ Let older children hide the afikoman for younger children or for the adults to find.

❖ Encourage participants to listen to Passover songs online before the seder. With repetitive verses that build on one another, these songs are not hard to master and fun to sing along.

Visit **www.behrmanhouse.com/passover** for activities, games, crafts, songs, and to practice the Four Questions.

Seder Table Checklist

You'll need the following items for the seder table:

- ❏ A haggadah for each participant
- ❏ The prepared seder plate
- ❏ A plate with three matzot (plural of *matzah*), under a matzah cover
- ❏ Pillows or cushions for reclining
- ❏ Festive tablecloth, dishes, and silverware
- ❏ Candlesticks, candles, matches
- ❏ Wine glass for each person
- ❏ Wine and/or grape juice
- ❏ A pitcher of water, a bowl, and a small towel, for hand washing
- ❏ A dish of salt water, for dipping parsley
- ❏ Small bowls of extra parsley, charoset, and horseradish
- ❏ Elijah's Cup, an extra wine glass or goblet partly filled with wine
- ❏ Miriam's Cup, an extra wine glass or goblet filled with water

If you do not have ritual items such as a seder plate, matzah cover, and cups for Elijah and Miriam, feel free to create your own by decorating a special dish, cloth napkin, or wine glasses for that purpose. (*See page v.*)

The Passover Meal

Preparing a seder meal is different from planning a dinner party, in part because of the ritual foods involved. Here are some tips.

Planning the menu

Ask friends and relatives for favorite Passover recipes, and remember to adjust them for the number of people you expect to have at your seder, as well as any special dietary needs. Don't forget traditional foods like matzah ball soup or gefilte fish. Some seder hosts set out vegetables or hard-boiled eggs for guests to snack on after saying the blessing over karpas.

Cooking in advance

Some items can be cooked in advance and frozen, such as brisket or matzah balls. Not all recipes freeze and reheat well, so choose carefully. When you shop, remember to stock up on Passover essentials such as matzah, matzah meal, gefilte fish, and wine or grape juice.

Preparing the seder plate

You will need to buy or prepare the following foods for the seder plate. You can read about their significance on pages 4-5 of this haggadah.

- ◆ **Karpas:** usually a sprig of parsley, but some families use another green vegetable or a potato.

- ◆ **Beitzah:** A roasted egg. You can roast a boiled egg in the oven until the shell starts to brown.

- ◆ **Maror:** A bitter herb, usually a piece of horseradish root or a small scoop of ground horseradish from a jar.

- ◆ **Zeroa:** A roasted lamb shank bone, which you can request from the butcher in your supermarket or butcher shop. A chicken bone is sometimes substituted. Vegetarians may use a roasted beet instead.

- ◆ **Charoset:** A sweet mixture of fruit, wine, and nuts. Families of Eastern European (Ashkenazic) descent usually use chopped apples, walnuts, and wine. Charoset from other regions and traditions may include dates, figs, apricots, bananas, and other ingredients. Charoset is best made 1-2 days in advance, to deepen the flavor (and give it that brown, mortar-like appearance!).

- ◆ **Chazeret:** An optional second bitter herb, such as romaine lettuce. Not all seder plates have a place for chazeret.

 Visit **www.behrmanhouse.com/passover** for recipes and more planning tools.

Planning Checklist

Use this checklist to plan your seder, from special foods, to activities for children, to the length and content of the seder service. By planning ahead, you'll make seder preparation easy, keep track of all the details, and avoid a last-minute rush.

One or two weeks before:

❑ Plan your menu • *see page iii*

❑ Make your shopping list and start cooking • *see page iii*

❑ Be sure you have a haggadah for each participant

❑ Check that you have a seder plate, candlesticks, and special cups for Elijah and Miriam • *see page iv*

❑ Plan activities for children • *see page v*

❑ Plan your seder service • *see page vi*

❑ Invite guests to prepare something to share during the seder • *see page vi*

Two or three days before:

❑ Prepare the foods for the seder plate • *see page iii*

❑ Defrost foods that were previously cooked and frozen

❑ Be sure you have a reward for guests (usually children) who find the afikoman • *see page vi*

The night before:

❑ Prepare the seder plate • *see page iii*

❑ Set the table • *see page iv*

❑ Search for chameitz • *see page vii*

The day of:

❑ Finish preparing your meal . . . and don't forget the matzah ball soup!

❑ Set out the seder plate and other ritual foods, and pour the wine or grape juice

❑ Have fun!

Simply Seder

Planning Your Passover Seder

Edited by Dena Neusner
Illustrated by Julie Wohl

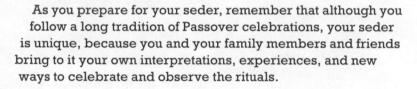

Turn over for your **Passover Haggadah**

The Jewish people have celebrated Passover together since the Israelites left Egypt more than three thousand years ago. From generation to generation, on the fifteenth day of the Jewish month of Nisan, Jews around the world hold a seder designed to help us feel as if we were there with our ancestors in ancient Egypt, so that we will always remember the story of our people's journey from slavery to freedom.

As you prepare for your seder, remember that although you follow a long tradition of Passover celebrations, your seder is unique, because you and your family members and friends bring to it your own interpretations, experiences, and new ways to celebrate and observe the rituals.

On the following pages, you will find useful tools, ideas, and checklists for planning your seder. You can find more resources online. When it's time to start the seder, simply flip over the book for a complete Passover haggadah.

Use your smartphone to discover more Passover resources.

BEHRMAN HOUSE

 Visit **www.behrmanhouse.com/passover** for blessings, songs, recipes, activities, and games.